Paul Bowles

SONATA
for Two Pianos

ED 4070

First Printing: March 1998

ISBN 0-7935-9277-1

G. SCHIRMER, *Inc.*

DISTRIBUTED BY

 **HAL•LEONARD®**
CORPORATION

7777 W. BLUEMOUND RD. P.O. BOX 13819 MILWAUKEE, WI 53213

for Arthur Gold and Robert Fizdale

SONATA

Paul Bowles

I

II

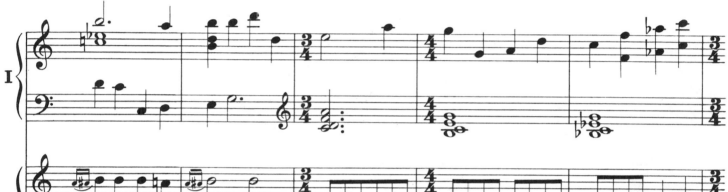

19

prominent

III

Absolutely strict tempo ♩ = 66

sempre senza pedale e staccato

Absolutely strict tempo ♩ = 66

sempre senza pedale e staccato

(slow crescendo from here to end)

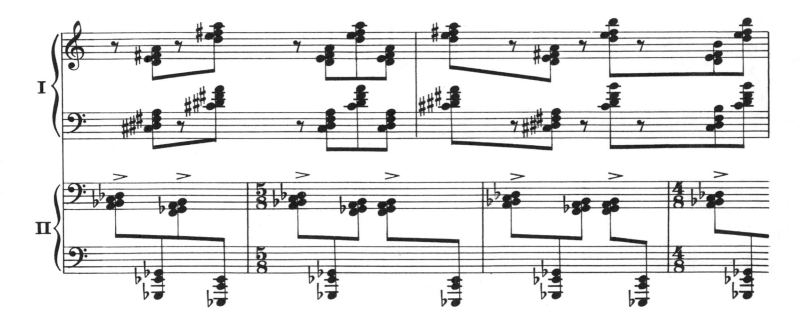

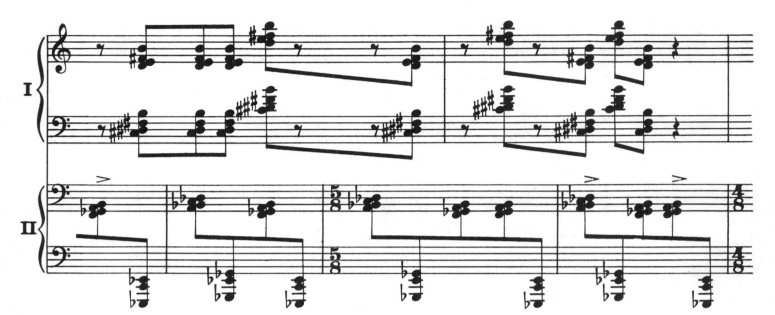

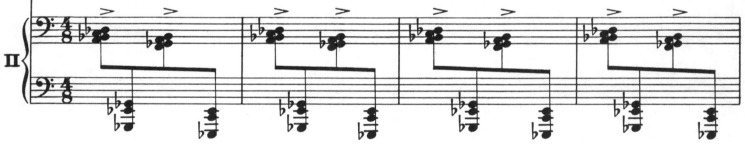

Tempo I°

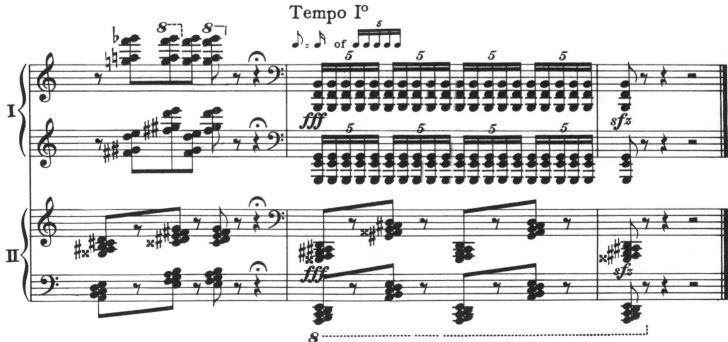